Rising Up

Out of

Chaos

'Reflections on the Book of Ezra'

JOURNEY ALONGSIDE THE ISRAELITES AS THEY RETURN
FROM CAPTIVITY TO REBUILD THEIR BROKEN LIVES

By Nicholas D'Acquisto

RISING UP OUT OF CHAOS

ISBN-13: 978-0692964590
ISBN-10: 0692964592

Cover Artwork: Sara D'Acquisto

Contact Information: Nicholas D'Acquisto
dacquistofamily@yahoo.com
www.dacquistofamily.wordpress.com

Rising up out of Chaos

About The Author

Nicholas D'Acquisto was born February 19, 1978 to James and Julie D'Acquisto. He was raised in the Central Valley of California in the small agricultural town of Visalia. He married his beautiful bride, Sara, in the year 2000. That same year, he began leading small groups and churches in worship before moving to Georgia to assist with a new church plant for a few years. He was ordained in 2008 by the Vineyard Churches and served in Central California as a pastor for five years. In 2013, he moved with his family to serve as missionaries in Northern Haiti with an organization that is home to over 100 children, has a medical center for the community, a school, and a church for the surrounding town. Haiti is one of the most economically devastated and socially bruised countries in the world. Nick and his family's great joy has been found loving those who are without - especially those without a Mom or Dad.

He wrote this book during his time living and working among the people of Haiti. Nick and his wife continue that work today serving with an organization advocating for children in need around the world.

Rising up out of Chaos

Contents

BOOK DEDICATION

This book is lovingly dedicated to Christla (*Christ-is here*) and to all the other children of Haiti who must 'rise up out of chaos' just to live - my hat goes off to each of you. You are forever in my heart!

Christla, even though you are a small child right now, what you have already overcome in life is tremendously big - you are a shining light to us all!

ACKNOWLEDGMENTS

My deepest thanks to my wife Sara for conversing daily with me
about all the subjects in this book, for allowing me the time to
write, and for praying through all of life with me.
You are an amazing woman of God!

I'm grateful for Anna, Halley, Asher and Christla who daily inspire
me to become a better father and man.

Thank you Mom, for all your editorial work in helping me write
this book. Your school teacher wisdom improved this work greatly.
Thank you Papa and Jeff Kenny, for doing early read throughs, and
for reminding me that each of these chapters are pastoral sermons
in print. Thank you to all the missionaries I have served alongside
in Haiti, and the other ministers of the gospel of Jesus that I have
been privileged to work with in my life.

I am grateful to all those along the way who helped me become
who I am, for we can only write from the foundations
of who we are. To God be the glory!

Thank you.

INTRODUCTION

I have loved the book of Ezra for a number of years. Something about it spoke to my heart the first time I read it, and it seems that whenever I find myself in the midst of life-type chaos, this book finds its way back to my mind and heart. There is something about the nature of this story that intrigues me. It captures a spirit of rising up out of chaos - a people rising when they should be falling, and succeeding when they should be failing. We all go through times like these and we all need God given stories, like Ezra, to show us there is a way out of the chaos.

The book of Ezra recounts the historical journey of the exiled Jews returning to Jerusalem to rebuild their lives after a horrific time of captivity in Babylon. King Nebuchadnezzar originally took the Israelites into captivity in 586 B.C., and when King Cyrus came into power, he issued a decree allowing the Jewish people to return. There was a first group sent back under a man named Zerubbabel to rebuild the temple to God, and a later group sent back under a man named Ezra to re-establish the laws of God.

This second great exodus from Babylon to Jerusalem is often overlooked by popular Bible studies and children's stories; but contains a most treasured movement of God's people that weave together Old Testament leaders, priests, prophets, and common people who were leaving their foreign lands behind to return to their cherished homeland in God.

Lately, I have been back in this Ezra book, learning again in this season of life how to come out of my own chaos. My father passed away from cancer just before my wife and I and our three children left for Haiti. This left a deep sadness in my heart and quite honestly, it left me feeling exposed as a man. There is a certain covering and protection that a father gives you. It is a tough reality for each of us to bear when we realize that we too are not immune to tragedy, loss, and brokenness - time and circumstance happen to us all. It is in the aftermath of these times that we begin to look around us for glimpses of hope, for stories like Ezra with broken people rising again, and for people around us who are able to move past these difficult seasons with more ease than us.

I wrote the basic chapters of this book while living in Haiti - one of the most economically devastated and socially bruised countries in the world. The people of Haiti seem to inherently know that brokenness is a part of life, and it allows them to move forward more easily than the rest of us. There is a quiet strength I see

14

among the people of Haiti, mostly among the children, and it has taught me more than I could ever fully describe and has given me a deep hope in my own life for the goodness of God.

> 'The Lord is near to the brokenhearted
> and saves the crushed in spirit.'
> Psalm 34:18

My hope in writing this is to show that *'rising up out of chaos'* is possible for you and me. We long as a people for examples, for stories that show us how to live our lives. We need something to look at, something or someone to imitate, a mentor to guide us out of our own foreign lands and back to our homeland in God - the Bible is full of these trusted stories and the entire book of Ezra points us in this way towards God deliverance.

As I have sat with the book of Ezra for many long hours and days and slowly pulled back the layers, I found this book to be divided into three major sections that I will call; The Primary Stages, The Outer Stages and The Inner Stages of our lives. The words I have written in this book are not meant to be a complex historical breakdown or biblical commentary on the book of Ezra; rather, I have sought to pull upon spiritual lessons that lead to our recovery as a people. The book of Ezra brilliantly leads us through these simple stages and spiritual lessons to places of victory if we let it.

These stages form the basis of this book as detailed below.

1. **The Primary Stages:** Chapter 1 of Ezra and the historical setting begin with the primary issues of *Our Heart* and *Our Belief*.

2. **The Outer Stages:** Chapters 2 - 5 of Ezra deal with those things in the external parts of our lives; *Our Relationships, Our Altars, Our Enemy,* and *Our Prophets*.

3. **The Inner Stages:** Chapters 6 - 10 of Ezra take us into the final and deep inner places of our personalities where God works out *Our Finish, Our Selves, Our Humility, Our Prayer,* and *Our Fight*.

As you may have noticed, each chapter begins with the word 'Our' to give emphasis to the fact that ownership is a key part of rising up above anything in this life. As long as we put the burden of responsibility on someone else, we will never move forward in life. Crucial to our maturity as men and women is to realize that our life is 'Our' responsibility. Much of my own learning in this area has come from Henri Nouwen in his book, Reaching Out;

My own deep-rooted fear to be on my own and alone kept me going from person to person, book to book and school to school, anxiously avoiding the pain of accepting the responsibility for my own life...

The time seems to have come when I can no longer stand back with the remark, 'Some say, others say,' but have to respond to the question, 'But what do you say?'

While our lives are 'Our' responsibility, we also recognize that without the power and strength of our risen Lord Jesus, no forward movement will ever be achieved. I have ended each chapter with a prayer to serve as an example of how one might honestly talk to God and ask for His indwelling power in each of these areas. These prayers are not meant to take the place of one's actual prayers which are deeply personal and life-changing.

I invite you to join me in this journey of Rising Up Out of Chaos; a most beautiful and God-directed path that we must all take many times over in this journey of life. None of us are exempt, and my prayer is that the sacred book of Ezra and the words written herein will be of some help in bringing your life from chaos to beauty!

RISING UP OUT OF CHAOS

SECTION I: THE PRIMARY STAGES

OUR HEART
OUR BELIEF

OUR HEART

Chapter 1 of Ezra finds King Cyrus giving a decree for the Jewish exiles to return to their homeland from Babylon, thus fulfilling the long-awaited prophecy of Jeremiah.

'While he was still a long way off, his father saw him and felt compassion, and ran and embraced him.'

Luke 15:20

What if you knew that your heart was God's most prized possession? Not what you could ever do for Him, just plain and simple - you. What if you really knew this, what if you really believed this? I believe we will search all our lives until we finally find this true love of the Father. Ezra chapter 1 subtly, yet beautifully, leads us to discover this.

The book of Ezra has a most interesting beginning, it doesn't even begin with Ezra, in fact, we don't see him until chapter 7; the book of Ezra begins with another character working 'behind the scenes' to *stir* and move the hearts of Jeremiah, Cyrus and the Israelites. This character is titled 'Lord' and 'God' and He begins His work by stirring people to do things instead of doing things himself. Take a look at the opening verses of Ezra chapter 1.

'In the first year of Cyrus king of Persia, that the word of the Lord by the mouth of Jeremiah might be fulfilled, the Lord <u>stirred up</u> the spirit of Cyrus... Then rose up... everyone whose spirit God had <u>stirred</u> to go up to rebuild the house of the Lord that is in Jerusalem'

Ezra 1:1 & 5

How strange right? Why does God stir hearts instead of just take care of things Himself? Have you ever thought about why God involves us in His work on earth? I believe He is after so much more than we think - I see a Great Father inviting us into His work so He can forge a deeper work in our hearts. I know from my understanding of the rest of the Bible that God is after more than Jeremiah could ever prophesy, Cyrus could ever decree, what any of the Israelites could ever rebuild, and what you and I could ever do. His goal is always to impart His love deep within us.

From an early age, I can remember helping my Dad and brother work on our cars; in fact, we worked on *all* our cars. My Dad would refuse at all costs ever taking the car to a shop. He was a mechanic and whatever the problem, whatever the noise, the answer was simple, "pull it in the garage and let's take a look." The cars were many and remain a blur in my mind, but what I *do* remember is how I felt on the inside when my Dad would ask me to help him fix these cars. I recall him saying things like, "Nick, can you hold the flashlight so I can see down there and re-connect that hose" or "my hand is just too big, can you see if you can get your hand in there and grab that bolt that dropped?" These things sound so simple as I write them, but they were huge for me as a little boy. I was being invited by my Dad to keep the family car working.

Through this process I felt important, I felt needed, and I felt proud inside that *I* was being asked to help. The cars would get fixed and another week or two would go by and the process would be repeated. But, during those simple tasks of keeping our family moving on all four wheels, a far bigger task was being completed in my heart -

Knowing I was special to my Dad.

I believe God stirs our hearts to accomplish things for the same reason - to remind us of His love for us. Some of us didn't have this kind of upbringing from an earthly father; some of us used to have it, but time and circumstances have changed things. I wish I could hear my own Dad's voice ask me just one more time to come and help him - I would jump at the chance. I lost him a little over two years ago and the emptiness is still real, but my heart remembers the way he fathered me into adulthood. Each of our stories is different, but we all long for Father love in its most primal form and we will continually search for it until we find it.

'You have made us for yourself O Lord,
and our hearts are restless until they rest in you.'
St. Augustine of Hippo

I am not sure where life has you today or what chaos lies in or around you, but the first great step forward is to know that the Father loves you and thinks the world of you! Yes, He will stir your heart and ask you to step into great and mighty assignments, but never allow yourself to stop with the work alone, for the heart is always more important than the work. He loves you for who you are, not what you do. Don't misunderstand me, what you *do* in life matters, it matters immensely, but He longs to *know you* in a loving relationship above all.

So, the book of Ezra begins, it begins with God and not with us, it begins with this same 'behind the scenes' character called 'Lord' and 'God'. This God who will never stop loving you, pursuing you beckoning you, and stirring you. This God who will continually be working behind the scenes of your life, in and through all your intricate circumstances, to establish His beautiful love inside your heart - and to remind you, that you are special.

Thank you Father, for your great love for me, even when I seemingly fail - your love for me never changes. Thank you for leading me through this life which has been tough at times. Please grow me in those areas where I still struggle to know you are proud of me and love me. Help me to fully realize that I am fearfully and wonderfully made by You.

Amen.

CHAPTER 2

OUR BELIEF

Ezra chapter 1 (continued) calls us to remember the historical setting of this great book; an exiled people waiting on the fulfillment of a 70-year prophecy from Jeremiah so they can return to their homeland after captivity.

"All things are possible for one who believes."
Jesus speaking to a struggling father - Mark 9:23

Before we get too far into Ezra we find ourselves asking, 'Why did all this have to happen in the first place, why are the Israelites returning to their old home to rebuild anyways?' Well, a long time before the book of Ezra was written there were many kings, and unfortunately, we wouldn't need books like Ezra if those kings had been good kings. But they got themselves and their kingdoms into

so much wickedness that after years and years of God's mercy, Hi
hand was forced to move them into captivity. In the summer of 58
B.C., King Nebuchadnezzar captured the famed city of Jerusalem
burned their sacred temple, and ordered survivors be taken
captive to Babylon. A terrible time for sure; Solomon's beautifull
ornate temple designed by David himself - now in ruins.

It is here, in the midst of this chaotic mess of captivity that the
book of Ezra finds its historical setting. It was during this time tha
the prophet Jeremiah arose, birthing a famous message from Go
to the broken children of Israel;

*"When **seventy years** are completed for Babylon, I will come to you and*
fulfill my gracious promise to bring you back to this place (Jerusalem).
For I know the plans I have for you," declares the Lord, "plans to prospe
you and not to harm you, plans to give you hope and a future.'
Jeremiah 29:10-11 (New International Version)

The entire book of Ezra is based upon this very promise - thi
exact prophecy - the fulfillment of *this* belief. That after 70 year
God would come, the captivity would be over and the people coul
return to their homeland of Jerusalem.

Now many of us know the latter part of this verse (*For I know th*
plans I have for you...), but we forget the struggle and waiting thes

28

people went through, as notated at the beginning of this verse, to earn this privilege of God. 70 years is a long time to wait and believe that God will move on your behalf! I can only imagine the depth of anguish these people experienced trying to hold onto this hope that felt so far away.

You may be in the middle of some anguished place as well right now, trying to cling to hope. The enemy may be speaking harmful words to your soul like *'it will always be like this'* or *'things will never change.'* For most of us, these thoughts and feelings are the basis of our worst depressions, frustrations, and inner anger. Wanting to go forward, but not being able to move.

It is difficult to move our hearts beyond this hopeless place when we find ourselves here; I must admit, my own heart has spent way too much time in places of unbelief. The only time things have truly changed for me are when I have engaged my Father in heartfelt prayer and told Him how I'm really doing on the inside. Similar to the anguished father crying out to Jesus in Mark 9:24, *"help my unbelief!"* I acknowledge my spiritual weakness before Him, and then I wait to hear from Him. I truly wait in silence until I hear Him break through all the other voices in my head and speak to my heart. That is where the healing happens.

Eight months before moving to Haiti, I remember God giving Sara and I a symbol of victory, something to keep in front of us to look forward to in our journey - a 70 year prophecy if you will. We had clearly heard God's call to come to Haiti but we were still struggling with a lot of doubt and fear about uprooting our family and moving to an impoverished country. The house where we would be moving to in Haiti had a big black metal gate that entered from the dirt street. We began calling this door the *Black Gate of Victory*. Knowing that one day, if we continued to believe, we would arrive through that gate with our family in Haiti. It became a symbol for us, something to hold onto when things seemed dark. Little did I know how important that symbol would become to us.

It was a month later we found out my Dad had terminal cancer. This turned the next 2 months into a myriad of hospital visits and gut-wrenching pain as we ministered to him and watched his life ebb away that winter; he died on the first day of spring. The weeks and months that followed had a lot of internal pain for me and effort trying to console my Mom, but still in the silent moments we continued to see the Black Gate in front of us. It was my Mom's voice that summer that brought some clarity to me; out of her own place of pain she said to me, "It's ok, I know you're supposed to move to Haiti, that's where God is leading you."

After moving past many more struggles; raising support, leaving my job, renting our house out, selling our minivan, loaning my truck out, and getting 5 people's lives packed up in suitcases, we finally made it to the Black Gate of Victory in early August of 2013. Tears streamed down Sara and I's faces as we walked off the dirt road and through that Black Gate with our family. It was a moment of victory because we had faced so much opposition to just getting there. I remember speaking to the enemy in that moment, 'God wins and you lose!' This enemy who had caused me so much pain and anguish in this process, this enemy who was clearly defeated through simple faith and perseverance would now have to take a backseat to God's plan.

Maybe you're in some type of waiting place right now. Yours may not be 70 years, but maybe it's been a year or two that you have waited. Don't give up! God has spoken to you, given you a promise - and that is a beautiful treasure to hold on to. The key is learning to live in the middle of your 70 years like the end has already happened - and prophetically speaking, it has! Fight the internal discouragement and set your heart's belief to live in the mindset that it's already finished. This is the kind of faith that has risen above difficulties to build schools, start churches, heal marriages and rescue children - but it starts with belief.

Maybe this is a time of pause for you, a time to give your waiting up to the Lord. Let this be a place to stop and reflect on how He has been faithful so far in your life, and then ask Him for the strength to keep trusting and believing Him.

And remember that prophecy of 70 years from Jeremiah? It was exactly 70 years from the destruction of the first temple (586 B.C.) to the finished building of the second temple (516 B.C.); just as God said through Jeremiah before it ever even happened. They needed only believe, as do we! His timing is always perfect.

"Blessed are those who have not seen and yet have believed."
Jesus - John 20:29

<u>PRAYER</u>

God, you know my constant struggle to believe you are working out your good plan in my life. I confess that my eyes of faith and belief often grow dim in the waiting seasons of life. I want to feel hope again deep down inside; remind me through the simple activities of my day that all of life is a treasure and that hope in what you are doing is not some far off thing, but it is right here in front of me. Heal my heart in this area God. Restore my heart to trust and believe you again.

Amen.

RISING UP OUT OF CHAOS

CHAPTER 3

OUR RELATIONSHIPS

Ezra 2 documents the names of the actual people who returned from exile in Babylon and resettled in Jerusalem and Judah.

"We have been created for greater things, not just to be a number in the world, not just to go for diplomas and degrees, this work and that work. We have been created in order to love and be loved."
Mother Teresa

During World War II, over 400,000 Jewish prisoners at the Auschwitz Concentration Camp were given a number by which they were referred to for administrative ordering. There is still record today of these large lists of un-named Jewish people during the holocaust. In time and all history, this numerical classifying of people and the brutal murder of an estimated 6 million human beings by the Nazi Regime remains one of the most cruel and evil acts to ever happen on earth. And what do we find at the root of this evil?

They were not treated, named, or cared for as *actual* people.

They were given a numbered tattoo upon their chest or forearm to distinguish them instead of their name. And sadly, when people are not named, we don't internally recognize their significance and importance as living people.

But upon naming, we enter relationship - and upon relationship we begin to love.

In the Bible, we find many large lists as well; lists with family names and the number of people in each family, but these lists are different than concentration camp lists, they give name and meaning to those involved instead of just a number.

In Ezra chapter 2 we find such a list - it is of the first group of exiles returning from Babylon under the leadership of Zerubbabel to resettle in Jerusalem and Judah. We find beautiful names like Arah of the tribe of Asher; and Adin, whose name means delicate. We find out in the book of Nehemiah that this delicate man, Adin became a chief among his people and even put his name to the covenant with God established under Nehemiah. Maybe God needed a delicate and kind-hearted leader for his recovering people. The point is clearly made though, these people are named because they matter.

So many of us, myself included, in search of our own importance and significance make 'numbers' of the people around us instead of naming and knowing them. Ezra reminds us this is *not* good. It is both important and holy work to give significance and meaning to the people around us, *to name the un-named* in our lives.

How beautiful it is to work at just knowing the people in our lives, to make the insignificant known, to make large those that are small in our world. We must slow down and *see* those who are right before us; sadly, this is most often the people in our own family and neighborhoods. We must move beyond 'hello' and engage ourselves in the incredible stories of those sitting around our dinner tables, those taking up the seats next to us, and those on our streets. In doing so, not only do we help to recover their identity, but we strangely recover our own.

When I turn to God in prayer over the sadness I often feel in my own heart, I am reminded by God how blessed I am with the beautiful people around me. Jesus appeared to us as Immanuel (God with us), and made each person around Him significant by

being with them and noticing them, especially the broken an
downcast. In word and deed Jesus lived this out - and because c
this, He carried a secret joy deep in his heart. We need onl
recognize that each living person around us is created in the imag
of God and treat them as holy and God-created individuals.

A beautiful reminder to me of this very thing is our daughte
Christla's name. In Haitian Creole, the word 'la' means 'here'. So
her name, Christ-la, literally means, *'Christ is here!'* What could b
simpler than seeing the beauty of Jesus in every single life.

Sadly, when we don't recognize this, it can have devastating effec
on those around us, especially when it's our children that we don
see Jesus in. When we are unwanted by those who should b
caring for us the most, it is a most evil thing.

I remember exiting our house one afternoon in Haiti and seeing
little girl, about 3 years old, standing on the dirt road crying. Sh
was all alone and I looked up and down the street and couldn
find who she belonged to. She said she didn't know where h
mom was. A friend of mine approached and asked if I needed hel
with her. I stayed with the girl but asked him to go and ask on th
main street to see if anyone knew where this girl's mom was.

He eventually came back with the mom and she quickly began

reprimand the little girl for following her to the market; apparently the mom hadn't known she was following her and the girl had lagged behind and gotten lost on our street. The mom, who had a few other kids with her, then turned to me and asked if I wanted the little girl?!? I was initially stunned and then said to the mom, "I cannot take this child, you are the best person who could ever care for this child as her mom." She looked at me with disgust and then at the child with a similar disgust, grabbed her arm and walked off.

I felt sad for this mom who I could see was struggling to care for her family, but I felt most sad for this child who was unwanted by her mom. I tried to encourage the mom to love her daughter and care for her, I only hope my words sank in though as I never saw her or the child again. Being unwanted is a most terrible thing.

When we moved to Haiti, I didn't realize I would come into contact with so many who fell into this category of the orphaned and unwanted. Currently, my wife and I are the house parents of 28 girls here in northern Haiti - 28 treasured daughters of God. Coming from a solid parent situation myself, I can honestly say I do not know what these children have been through. But *I can* offer the covering and strength of a father to them. And the grand statement of Jesus to *'love your neighbor as yourself'* (Matthew 39:40) comes alive before my very eyes. Somehow, we all know deep inside that the secret to true joy is found in opening ourselves up to love another human being.

May we never digress again to not *truly* knowing those around us for in choosing to 'name' the un-named, we make a step forward out of the chaos of all our lives. Chaos, by definition is complete disorder and confusion. Naming and knowing the people in our midst moves us from chaos to order, from unknown to known, and from unloved to loved. What could be simpler than just loving those around us. As Heidi Baker, missionary to Mozambique said "*Ministry... is simply loving the person in front of you.*"

May it be so among us.

PRAYER

Jesus, I am so grateful you have shown me that by simply loving you and opening my life up to those around me I can lead a beautiful and rich life. It is so simple, yet I complicate it so easily. Take me back to the basics of just loving the one you bring in front of me each day. Forgive me for all those you brought in front of me that I let pass by without taking the time to see your beauty in them. Lead me to love as you do.

Amen.

CHAPTER 4

OUR ALTARS

Ezra 3 details the rebuilding of the altar in Jerusalem and the foundations of a new temple.

'He leads me beside still waters. He restores my soul.'
David - Psalm 23:2-3

It wasn't much, but it was everything all at the same time. The Hebrew altar was essentially just some nicely cut stones with a fire grate on top - but to the Israelites, it was *everything!* They had not been able to keep the morning and evening sacrifices alongside their Babylonian captors for quite some time; no feast days, no worship services, no holy celebrations without an altar. The actual temple building would be another few years in the making now that they had returned. But first, Zerubbabel and Jeshua led the

41

people in building a simple altar that stood separately, just outside where the temple would be.

Simple, but incredibly needed. Foreigners now back home, finding their way out of the chaos and rebuilding their lives. What do they begin with, where do they start?

With their altar of worship.

Often times we find ourselves in foreign lands, among foreign peoples and our own altars of worship somehow get removed from their places too. These foreign places can be geographic or they can be a period in our lives of confusion or chaos, or possibly of losing something or someone we dearly loved. Sometimes we can't even put our finger on things, it is just the realization that deep inside, something is not right. We feel scattered instead of complete. Worn out instead of alive. Lost in a vast world of emptiness and afraid we will never be noticed, found or loved.

There is some strange footing we all lose at different points in our lives. How do we move on? How do we get back to clarity and completeness? The message of Ezra 3 is clear - *Rebuild* your altar.

And the first of all altars is right inside your own heart.

Rebuilding our altars means making time for God again.

It means seeking His Presence above all other pursuits.

It means learning to pray and to worship again.

It means learning to listen for the quiet sound of His voice again.

It means opening up His Word for the sole purpose of waiting for Him to speak, just to you.

'Earnestly I seek you; my soul thirsts for you; my flesh faints for you, as in a dry and weary land where there is no water.'

Psalm 63:1

Our soul, at its core, thirsts for the Living God; yet we often try to quench it with everything else. In our cramped society, our minds have so many things we can choose to focus on and delve into, there almost seems no end to the many pursuits we can engage ourselves in. This world is filled with endless activities, but only one pursuit is necessary for the wholeness of our hearts.

One of my favorite ways to find escape from these endless activities is to head to the mountains where I can be in the stillness among God's untouched creation. There I find my own altar to God, the place where I come back to just being alone with Him. There my heart is at rest and peace again.

An altar is simply a place where you meet with the Living God and

He meets with you. We all intrinsically know what our altar to God looks like, we just rarely make time for it in our busy lives.

I love that the Israelites chose to build their altar as their first act of rebuilding their homes and lives - may it be the same with us.

PRAYER

God, you know how easily distracted I get from the most important thing in life - just being alone with you. Give me the grace to rebuild my own altar, it has lost its place in my life too many times. God, I love you and want to be with you more; to hear from you, to speak with you. You are the only one who can quench this deep thirst within me. Lead me back to my own altar where I can find lasting joy in you again.

Amen.

CHAPTER 5

OUR ENEMY

Ezra 4 finds the Israelites encountering opposition as they try to rebuild their temple.

'When I want to do right, evil lies close at hand.'
Paul - Romans 7:21

Many people I talk to who come visit our facility in Haiti ask me what it's like to live in an impoverished country and what struggles I face. Usually it's just small talk they're after, and I answer with my basics like missing hot showers and food from my favorite restaurants. But every now and then, someone comes along who really wants to understand the actual spiritual battles my family and I face. I love to enter into these great conversations as these things are heavy on my heart. It doesn't matter if your mission field

45

is on your block or in another part of the world - the real struggle happening to people stepping out in faith is that they're encountering evil - real evil in its various forms. These attacks happen differently to each person; but from my own experience and in talking with others, the battle usually involves loneliness, feeling deserted and discouraged, attacks on your children, rejection from the people you're trying to reach, and nagging feelings that nothing is going to come of all your work, in spite of all you've given up. Mission work is hard work - it is light entering a dark place, and that will always bring opposition.

Turns out, that while the returned exiles were doing their difficult mission work of rebuilding the temple of God in Jerusalem, they found themselves in the presence of the enemy as well. Local leaders, without apparent knowledge of King Cyrus' earlier decree for the Israelites to return and rebuild were causing much distress.

'Then the people of the land <u>discouraged</u> the people of Judah and made them <u>afraid</u> to build and bribed counselors against them to <u>frustrate</u> their purpose.'

Ezra 4:4-5

While they were endeavoring to bring light to their world by setting up a temple where God could be known and worshipped, their enemies were working hard to <u>discourage</u> them, make them

46

<u>afraid</u>, and <u>frustrate</u> their purpose. Three things that sound pretty familiar, don't they? The people of Jerusalem were being affected by three of the most harmful things that can happen to anyone in the pursuit of good.

Who among us hasn't worked tirelessly on something, only to be defeated in the end by discouragement? Who hasn't stayed in their safe place out of fear of what *might* happen? Who hasn't thrown their hands up in frustration? You can imagine the heartache these things would bring on an entire community of people; especially a community involved in such a great work. Jesus came to bring us abundant life, and these things from the enemy are the exact opposite! This entire chapter in Ezra gives multiple accounts over a large span of time in order to re-tell how much pain and struggle these people went through to actually rebuild this temple.

Wherever we shine beauty, ugliness will rear its head!

It is a proven biblical truth spoken of by many saints, missionaries, pastors, and leaders; whenever we endeavor to do good in Jesus' name, we invite spiritual attack and bring the enemy out of hiding. As Paul said of his own life when he decided to act upon God's leading to go up to Jerusalem, '*constrained by the Spirit, not knowing what will happen to me there, except that the Holy Spirit testifies to me in every city that imprisonment and afflictions await me.*' Acts 20:23.

Imprisonment and afflictions await me? Paul knew these thing were going to come before they happened because he wa sensitive to the Holy Spirit and understood how the enemy works.

Haven't you noticed that when you are seeking to bring light b trying to make a difference in this dark world, that evil sneaks u on you as well? That's how you know it's spiritual opposition Those middle of the night anxiety attacks out of nowhere, th internal discouragement, that dormant temptation that enter your mind, the pushback you receive, the doubting, the fear.. These are all the same things the Israelites faced in the book o Ezra, and our lives are no different. Living out our faith invite conflict from the enemy, but it doesn't mean we stop, it means w press on through the chaos.

'I press on to take hold of that for which Christ Jesus took hold of me.'
Philippians 3:12 (New International Version)

'We are afflicted in every way, but not crushed; perplexed, but not driver to despair; persecuted, but not forsaken; struck down but not destroyed'

II Corinthians 4:8-9

It doesn't matter where you live, what job you have or wha activities you're involved in - wherever there are people, there i mission work and missionaries are needed. Your mission fiel

48

awaits you right where you live and work. Look for injustice where you can impart God's grace, ways to love the unlovely, someone to mentor and disciple, ways to bless the poor, the fatherless, and the elderly. But know that things will get tough, because mission work is holy and hard work. It is light entering the darkness through people like you and me.

'You are the light of the world.'
Matthew 5:14

So keep fighting, keep praying, keep believing, keep doing good, keep loving others, and keep bringing the love of Jesus into this *'crooked and twisted generation, among whom you shine as lights in the world'* Philippians 2:15-16

PRAYER

God, you know how I desire to bring your light into this dark world. Clarify the assignments you want me to walk in, and put your protection around me and my family as we step out. Come, O God, and lead me into the holy work you have prepared for my life. Use me to encourage others, to instill faith, and to brighten lives.

Amen.

CHAPTER 6

OUR PROPHETS

Ezra 5 tells of two wonderful prophets doing what they do best;
prophesying, encouraging, and pushing people towards excellence.
The end result is work begins on the temple again.

'At times our own light goes out and is rekindled
by a spark from another person. Each of us has cause to think with deep
gratitude of those who have lighted the flame within us.'
Albert Schweitzer

Have you ever come to a place in your life where your own ears couldn't make out the Word of God very well anymore? Maybe you came to a place where you found yourself stuck, tired, lost, and quite honestly, just plain confused. There have been times in my life where I found myself so lost and confused that I couldn't figure

out what to do next or how to go on. It was in those direc
moments that God brought someone into my life to speak exactl
what I needed to hear. For reasons known only to God, He createc
His people to need each other. He gave us the priceless gift o
being able to receive life from another soul. We all need hope
strength, and courage spoken to us from time to time; in biblica
terms, this is called the gift of prophecy.

Ezra chapter 5 gives us a glimpse into one of these exact moment
of prophecy. This first group of exiles that had returned under the
leadership of Zerubbabel had the main task of rebuilding the
temple, but work on that temple was getting just too hard. And t
make matters even worse, they were being harassed by loca
leaders and a far-off ruling king who was forcing them to sto
building. Pulled at every end. Confused, afraid, and discouraged
What do they do now? How do they go on? They drop their heads is
discouragement and exhaustion, and head back home.

Arise the prophets in our lives to awaken our souls.

The background to this story in Ezra is actually found in Hagga
(Hag-i), a book found later in the Old Testament. The man Hagga
a prophet during this time, speaks to the people after they ha
given up on rebuilding the temple and encourages them t
continue the work. In fact, they had not only stopped building the

temple, but they were only focused on building their private homes. It seems that whenever our spiritual lives lose focus, we find ourselves turning selfishly inwards. So, the Lord moves the prophet Haggai to not only encourage them, but to speak in tough love terms as well in hopes that their lives will turn towards God once again. *(Note: The prophet Zechariah was another prophet during this same time giving similar encouragement.)* Listen in as the prophet Haggai speaks:

'Is it a time for you yourselves to dwell in your paneled houses, while this house lies in ruins?
Be strong all you people of the land, declares the Lord.
Work, for I am with you.'
Haggai Ch. 1-2

I love the strong, but loving language the person and prophet Haggai uses here; it's almost like you can see him privately holding the leaders Zerubbabel and Jeshua by the shoulders in a fatherly sort of way, saying, *'Come on guys, you're spending a lot of time working on your own houses, but the temple of God is over there in ruins - this is not good!'* Then, I can see him step back and publicly command all the people to continue this good work of rebuilding the temple.

This is the gift of the prophet; they can speak strongly, but with

53

love, and the end result is courage aroused in us, not a feeling of being demeaned. We find ourselves with inner strength again, the kind of strength to continue. Many of us have felt this from a loving person in our lives; someone who took the time to see our pain and then looked us in the eyes and spoke - and we knew in our hearts it was the voice of God. It takes courage to be a prophet in someone else's life, and it takes humility to hear it.

I remember back in 2004, my wife and I had been living in Augusta, Georgia for two years helping with a church plant. It was an exciting time for us of beginning ministry out of college, working to start something new, and networking with different pastors and leaders in the area. The problem was, after two years the church plant ended, and we found ourselves in a broken place of chaos wondering what to do next.

We had purchased a house in Georgia, had our first child Anna and I had begun full time work with a non-profit helping young people get into college and careers. We were far from our home and family in California though, and we were unsure how to proceed in life. We found ourselves very confused and it was causing a lot of stress in our lives. In our brokenness, we began attending a Vineyard church full of people who genuinely cared about us, it was here that God used a prophet in my life one night.

We had gathered as a small group on a Wednesday night for Bible study and worship. Afterwards, the men went to the dining room table to pray for each other and the women stayed in the living room. There were four of us men sitting together, and we each shared the things we were struggling with. I shared how broken we felt after the church plant ended, our lead pastor had moved on with his family, and we had now put our house up for sale as well. The problem was, we weren't sure if it was time to go back to California yet, God seemed to be doing a measure of healing in our hearts at this Vineyard church, but we really missed our home and family. We were just plain confused.

After I shared this, a man named Carlos, who I was just getting to know, very boldly looked me in the eyes and said, "Nick, your wife is going to very clearly tell you tonight what you need to do, don't say anything to her about this, just trust me that she will tell you tonight what needs to be done." I didn't know what to say to him. Quite honestly, I didn't really believe him at all because we had been struggling with what to do for a while now. But he said it three or four times in complete confidence that this would happen tonight.

That night as my wife and I were getting ready for bed and casually talking, she suddenly got quiet, looked me in the eyes and said, "Nick, we need to pull our house off the market here in

Georgia and stay here for this next season as God heals our hearts."

I was blown away and tears began to stream from my eyes as in that instant I remembered what Carlos had told me just hours earlier, and my wife doesn't usually speak like this. I then told her about Carlos' words and she began to cry too. That night, in the dark, near midnight, we went out to our front yard, pulled our For Sale sign out of the ground and did stay another year in Georgia which ended up being very crucial to our life and calling.

These brittle moments in our lives become the birthplace of the good and positive changes God desires in us. As I look back on specific points in my life, the most beautiful times were directly *after* one of these prophetic words was given to me; like God using Carlos and my wife to get through to me that night. It reset my heart compass on true north again and I had confidence to forge ahead on my life path. These things are recorded in my journal with a glad and smiling heart. We all need to hear words spoken to our soul from another person; for sometimes God must use a human voice to get through to us. It is one of his most beautiful and precious gifts.

God uses those around us... and we find peace and clarity again. We do things like stand still when people all around us are saying move. We're able to take risky steps towards rebuilding a broken relationship. We receive the faith to step into the unknown.

Listen carefully to the people who are speaking life into you, they mean well - you may even be surprised *who* God uses to speak to you!

'He who has ears to hear, let him hear.'
Luke 8:8

<u>PRAYER</u>

Lord, you know I struggle with confusion and loss of direction at times, I thank you for the gift of the people around me who are willing to speak truth into my life - even when it hurts. I thank you for sending me encouragement right when I need it. I treasure your voice God, I long to hear from you through your people. Strengthen me, bind up my weak areas and fit me for the race you have called me to run.

Amen.

RISING UP OUT OF CHAOS

CHAPTER 7

OUR FINISH

In Ezra chapter 6 the temple is finally completed.

'On account of a slight difficulty you give up
what you have undertaken
and are too eager to seek consolation.'
Thomas à Kempis

Tell me, how many things lie in your graveyard of unfinished projects, dreams, and ideas? How many times have you set out to accomplish something, only to have it die a slow death? Why is it so hard for us to finish things? Setbacks, struggles, laziness, too much time, costs too much - the list goes on. Mine is a sad story to note as well. I have too many books, blogs, and ideas that only made it to my journal, too many songs I never finished, and too

many house projects I never started. Did the ideas just get old, di
I get tired, did I just plain forget? I'm honestly not sure. Maybe yo
can agree.

It's easy to lose momentum as we forge through the strang
happenings and footings of our lives, especially when things ge
hard and difficult to finish. But when we give up in hopes c
finding peace and rest, we usually get the opposite reaction we ha
hoped for - feelings of defeat; especially if it was something Go
had put on our heart to do. Loss of achievement and purpose ca
plunge us into hopelessness and sometimes even depression. W
were created for finish. While every now and then it is ok t
abandon something that's not working, most of us need t
remember we weren't created to give up, we were created for finisl
Listen to some of those who have gone before us;

'I have fought the good fight, I have finished the race'
Paul speaking to Timothy - II Timothy 4:7

"My food," said Jesus, "is to do the will of him who
sent me and to finish his work."
John 4:34 (New International Version)

'It is finished.'
Jesus on the cross - John 19:30

Ezra chapter 6 holds a long-awaited moment of finality. After a literal time of blood, sweat and tears, the Israelites finally completed the temple. Ever since Ezra chapter 3, we have seen the many setbacks, problems, enemies and discouragement that they faced. Quite honestly, to them, I'm sure it appeared that this temple would *never* get done. I'm sure they started wondering, like we do, if God was even in this thing anymore. But then the beautiful and encouraging words of the prophets Haggai and Zechariah brought a breath of fresh air to the leaders and the people. They finally regained their strength to continue with what God had stirred them to do in the first place, and after 20 long years of hard work - the temple was finally completed!

Yes, it was tough.

Yes, it was draining at times.

Yes, it took a long time - but everything worthwhile usually does!

I remember a couple years back, my children had asked me to read them one of my favorite stories, Jean Craighead George's *My Side of the Mountain*. It's the story of a young boy who runs away to the wilderness and learns to survive off the land. I had started out reading them a chapter a night, but before long, tiredness set in and I found myself just saying goodnight to them and saying we'd read it tomorrow night. It wasn't even that difficult of a book either! I just lost my momentum. After some nights of not reading to them, something clicked in me as I thought about my kids one morning and the father I was called to be to them. I set my mind to finish this small task, and to this day, my kids still talk about that special reading time we had because I gave it importance and *my* finish.

This is a small example, but I want to stress the point that even small things are important before God if He puts them on your heart to do. There can certainly be large projects too - things that may take you years to complete, but size is not the issue, the issue is that God put it on your heart to do; and when you finish it, you will feel His joy!

> *'I consider my life worth nothing to me,*
> *if only I may finish the race and complete the task*
> *the Lord Jesus has given me.'*

Paul - Acts 20:24 (New International Version)

I wonder what temple projects lie in your path?

What does God desire to complete in your life?

What is it that needs *your* finish?

Rising out of chaos requires more than just hoping things will go well; sometimes it requires tears, sweat, and hard work. Just ask the Israelites. Be intentional to finish those small things in front of you, and watch how God multiplies that into a life of joy and purpose!

'He who began a good work in you will bring it to completion.'
Philippians 1:6

<u>PRAYER</u>

Father, you and I both know the many things you have laid upon my heart that never made it out of the gates - I know that your grace covers over a multitude of things, but I really want to finish the things you desire to complete in my life. Give me your wisdom to know which things to pick up and which things to let go of. I want to declare at the end of my life like Paul that I have fought the good fight and that I finished the race that you have given me to run.

Amen.

CHAPTER 8

OUR SELVES

80 years after the first group of exiles arrived back in Jerusalem,
Ezra was commissioned to return to Jerusalem from Babylon
and re-establish the laws of God.

'If you cannot make yourself what you would wish to be,
how can you bend others to your will?'
Thomas à Kempis

Ezra chapter 7 opens by finally introducing us to the man Ezra. Now, it may seem strange that we've been studying a book called Ezra and we still haven't met him. One of the more confusing parts to understanding the book of Ezra is realizing that there was an initial group that returned from Babylon under the leadership of Zerubbabel in order to rebuild the temple (chapters 1-6); and then there was a second group that came 80 years later under the leadership of Ezra in order to re-establish the laws of God (chapters 7-10). Ezra's purpose was different than Zerubbabel who came to rebuild a temple. Ezra's purpose was to teach the recovering people the ways of God. Ezra is described to us as scribe and priest who can trace his lineage back to Aaron the chief priest who was the brother of Moses. *Similar* to the story of Moses Ezra will find himself leading thousands of people on a long journey out of slavery and into freedom. 4-months and 900 miles of a journey from Babylon to Jerusalem to be exact!

The beautiful part about this chapter that I want to highlight is the clear glimpse we get into the inner life and character of Ezra, and how he led himself. Many of us have been to seminars on how to teach and lead others, how to influence and make organizational changes, but the *real* problem so many of us deal with is how to lead ourselves. We are everyone's best counselor, but we can't seem to counsel ourselves. So vastly important is the care we give our own souls. This key verse, Ezra 7:10, takes us past how Ezra led others, to how he led himself; and is our roadmap for personal spiritual growth.

'Ezra had set his heart to study the Law of the Lord, and to do it and to teach His statutes and rules in Israel.'

Ezra loved the Word of God more than anything else in life and had focused his heart to know and learn it above all other things. *'Ezra had set his heart to study the Law of the Lord.'* Have you ever set your heart to take on the beautiful task of learning, studying, and finding your life's continual direction in the Word of God? Now, I know belief in the Bible these days is fast becoming diluted in our communities and sadly, even our churches; but I can think of no greater way to measure our life and guide our steps through this dark world than with the Word of God. Oh, that we would set our hearts to study God's Word more earnestly like Ezra - drinking it in, meditating upon it, and letting it seep into our souls and guide our thinking. This is the basis of our deepest need; God himself re-aligning our minds with His truth, speaking to our hearts, and nourishing our souls.

My own learning in this area began when I was in my early twenties and in college. I couldn't get enough of the Bible; I would listen to sermons, read study books and devotionals, and immerse myself in the teachings of God. My heart still beats for God to speak to me through His Word, but there was a very definite and specific time when I was *first* learning about God through His Word - and it was very exciting! Still, my favorite thing to do first thing in the morning is to read a small section of the Bible and ask God, *'what are You speaking to me through this?'* Many times, the very thing I am working through and dealing with in life is answered by

69

God through these daily readings. It's my firm belief that God's 'word is a lamp to my feet and a light to my path.' Psalm 119:105. The Old Testament narratives pull me in and change me, the Psalms engage my emotions and bring healing, the words of Jesus draw me close to the Father, and the New Testament letters from the early church leaders re-align my thinking. It's so important to self feed upon the Word of God; we must seek Him ourselves like Ezra there will not always be a pastor or teacher to open up God's truth to us.

The second thing we find in this verse is four simple words that set the course for a life well lived and make Ezra stand out from so many other people across time and history: 'Ezra had set his heart to study the Law of the Lord, **and to do it.**' This tell-all fragment of a sentence says that not only did Ezra feed his own soul with God's Word, but he arranged the activities of his day 'to do' the things the Word of God was instructing him to do. He desired to 'live' a life of wholeness before God more than anything else. 'Be doers of the word, and not hearers only' James 1:22

One of the most healthy steps those of us rising out of places of internal chaos can do is to set a course for being 'intentional' about a few positive things in our lives as directed by God's Word. Maybe He's pulling you into deeper times of prayer or highlighting someone in your life that needs you right now. The key is intentionality on your part 'to do' the things He's leading you to do.

The third and, rightfully so, *last thing* we find in this verse is that: *'Ezra had set his heart to study the Law of the Lord, and to do it **and to teach his statutes and rules in Israel.**'* We study and do long before we are ever teachers. A great many people have set out to teach before their lives were truly ready to do so. It is from the overflow of a life well lived that our lives teach others.

In John Eldredge's book, Fathered by God, he discusses how a future king (young man) can be wounded when he is put in a position of authority way too young. For example; when a young youth pastor has to take over the entire leadership of a church because the senior pastor leaves, or when a father walks out on his family and leaves the 'son' to be the man of the house. Taking on leadership and teaching roles too early can wound a person's spirit because they don't have the maturity yet to handle this kind of responsibility.

Ezra didn't just arrive one day as chief leader, priest, and scribe. He got there by living these three things out day after day, and it's no different with us. Spend the vast amount of your time and energy nourishing your soul with God's Word, be intentional about following His ways as laid out in His Word, and then let the overflow of your life speak into and teach others.

<u>PRAYER</u>

Father, you know I long to grow as a person on the inside, to see my spiritual life move closer and closer towards what you desire for me. Help me grow in the way you long for my life to grow, I'm tired of trying to do things my way. Your Word is the best light for my path that I will ever have - help me to listen and trust you more fully.

Amen.

CHAPTER 9

OUR HUMILITY

Before the exiles depart on their 900-mile journey from Babylon to Jerusalem with their leader Ezra, they stop for something very important. Ezra Chapter 8 details this event.

'When you are older you will know that life is a long lesson in humility.'
J.M Barrie

There is a river just outside Babylon near the great Euphrates, known as the River Ahava. It is a smaller river, but just because it is small does not mean it is insignificant. In fact, some of the most beautiful things in life are the smallest and most often overlooked by people looking for the bigger and better. It was here at this River Ahava that something beautiful happened.

Ezra Chapter 8 begins with a list of thousands of Israelites wh
have gathered at the River Ahava to embark on a 4-month journe
of 900 miles from Babylon back to their homeland of Jerusalen
Ezra, who was leading this journey, had the difficult task of movin
these thousands of people back to their home country. At firs
glance, it seems that the great work was getting people from poir
A to point B, but at a closer look, we see that the great work wa
being done in the hearts of these people before they even left.

The moment itself actually came about rather humorously. Ezr
had proudly proclaimed to King Artaxerxes (the King of Persi
who commissioned Ezra) that they didn't need a guarded escoi
for the journey because they had God to protect them. But when
came time to leave, Ezra realized how dangerous these 900 mile
were actually going to be; fighting off thieves and bandits all th
way. Out of this place of feeling exposed and insecure about thi
great undertaking, and wishing he hadn't spoken so proudly i
front of the king, came something incredibly beautiful thougl
Ezra and all the people went to their knees in prayer at the Rive
Ahava, and in humility asked God to protect them.

'Then I proclaimed a fast there, at the River Ahava,
that we might humble ourselves before our God, to seek from Him a saf
journey for ourselves, our children, and all our goods.'
Ezra 8:21 & 23

In chapter 7 we learned about Ezra's true inner character and how he led himself, but it isn't until chapter 8 that we first see him in action; and what a beautiful moment it was. Asking thousands of people to kneel down by a river and humble themselves before God. It was here that a learned man became a spiritual leader, it was here that a brave man put down all his books, notes, and theories and became the humble leader God needed him to be.

I wish I could have been there to witness that amazing and holy moment - thousands of men, women and children on their faces before God in humility and prayer. If any one moment could be attributed to Ezra's success in rebuilding the nation of Israel - it would be this moment. It is rare for someone to practice this type of humility, especially a leader in a fearful situation - this is nothing short of heroic!

'All that has been said about humility is not enough to teach you humility. All that you have read about humility is not enough to teach you humility. You learn humility only by accepting humiliations. And you will meet humiliation all through your life.'
Mother Teresa

I've noticed that people have a lot to say about humility, but what I don't see is very many people practicing it. The humble ones among us are those probably not getting noticed or recognized for their achievements, because they've chosen to be ok without it. They are the ones who don't push their way up in a power-hungry world, because they've chosen to be ok *without* having to be on top - unless God ordains. They are the ones brave enough to let their pride go. They are the ones who find a simple beauty and relaxed peacefulness in just being themselves. Mostly, this kind of humility comes with going through difficult life experiences.

Living in Haiti among the poor and orphaned these last few years has brought me closer to humility than I've ever really been in my life. It has been my own personal time at the River Ahava. Before Haiti, everything in my life seemed to be about climbing up, striving after achievements, goals and success. I was working full-time as a Youth Program Manager for a large non-profit in downtown Fresno and part-time as an Associate Pastor at our church leading the night service. Something strange happened in me when we moved to Haiti though; I began to spend large amounts of time just loving and being among the children and people that live here. I found myself caring less about achievements and more about the people around me. I don't feel so driven to climb up the invisible ladder anymore; and it's not that I lost my drive for achievement altogether, it's just that I recognize my place among the community better - a community of beautiful and beautifully different people.

Humility comes from the Latin word *humilis*, which literally means low. Humility before God is recognizing ourselves as low, helpless and small before Him. It is also recognizing that we are not better than anyone else because of their financial, social, or emotional status. To recognize ourselves with the poor and lowly is to practice humility. False humility puts itself above others, often under the disguise of serving and helping; but true humility recognizes it is no different than anyone else - we *all* need God.

All of us on this journey out of chaos need time at the River Ahava, whether we go there ourselves or God sovereignly arranges for it, as He often does. Time at the River Ahava is that place where we stop being the leader, parent, pastor, coach, or teacher and simply become a child before God again. Humility re-aligns our heart before God and brings inner peace and freedom.

I am sure those 900 miles were much better off because of how Ezra led the people to begin this journey. It is no different with us - time at the River Ahava is needed before our own journeys can truly begin.

Father, help me to remember how much you love to see humility in my heart and life. I surrender my pride and personal drive to you - it often pulls me away from you. I don't want to succeed for my own personal gain, but simply to have you glorified in and through my life. Lead me down the courageous path of humility in this life, that I might be found close to you.

Amen.

CHAPTER 10

OUR PRAYER

In Ezra chapter 9, as we near the end of the book,
Ezra finds out that the returned exiles have broken trust with God
and sinned. Action will come later, but for now Ezra finds himself
with God in anguished prayer.

'It is impossible to carry on your life as a disciple
without definite times of secret prayer.'
Oswald Chambers

No chaos can ever be beaten by a strength that is but your own. If all you ever rely upon is yourself, you will rarely find your way out. Our greatest need is to know *we do* need help - that is the basis of prayer. This chapter, 'Our Prayer' follows closely after 'Our Humility' because they are both so interrelated they cannot be separated. The humble heart knows it needs God, and only the heart that knows it needs God can truly pray.

Lately, my 8 year old son Asher has been getting really frustrated at some things (school work, chores, etc.) that I see as simple - but to him, they are overwhelming and make him feel beaten down and crushed. I am trying to understand what's going on inside him though, to gently work with him and show him that when something is overwhelming he only needs to ask for help. I am also finding out that there is a lot of me in him - the weakness we see in our children most often lives in us as well. At times, I will beat my head against a wall in frustration trying to figure something out that would have only taken minutes had I stopped to ask for help. To understand this, is to understand prayer.

When we realize that we *can't do it* - and we *do* need God's help, our spiritual life begins to mature greatly. Until our life comes to this place of realizing our constant need for God each day, our prayer will simply be recitations of words, not a heart crying out in need.

Our chief character in this story, Ezra, shows us this kind of prayer in chapter 9. The very people he has been sent to lead are choosing a path that will destroy them and lead them away from God. They were commanded in Deuteronomy not to give their daughters in marriage to foreign men, and vice versa. *(This will b discussed more in the next chapter, Our Fight)* But Ezra has found this very thing happening among his people; he is broken by their sin and cries out in anguished prayer.

'I rose from my fasting, with my garment and my cloak torn, and fell upon my knees and spread out my hands to the Lord my God, saying: "O my God, I am ashamed and blush to lift my face to you, my God, for our iniquities have risen higher than our heads... Behold, we are before you in our guilt, for none can stand before you because of this."
Ezra 9:5-6 & 15

This is not prayers read from a book or simple recitations before bed, this is a man who earnestly needs God and His grace for himself and the people he is leading. Now, I understand not all prayers look like this, but in our neat society we have also turned our prayers into something far less than they were created to be.

'Lord, teach us to pray.'
Disciples speaking to Jesus in Luke 11:1

I remember a few years back during college I started a prayer journal after I heard a message on how important it was to break your journal and prayers into sections; one for what you're thankful for, one for your needs and one for your wants. At first, I enjoyed the organization of it, then it became really laborious and

81

hard for me to keep up with - in short, I began to resent my prayer time. What followed was a few years of frustrated prayer and not really feeling like I was getting anywhere or any closer to God through it.

It was actually after reading a certain book a few years later that God chose to restore my prayer life. In the book, the man spoke very conversationally with God, like he was speaking to a friend, not a method, not a form, not a stack of journals - just plain speaking with and listening to God. It was also around this same time that I read another great book by a famous Quaker Christian on listening to God. My life was simply revolutionized by these two books. I began to cherish my prayer times with God more than ever before because I was truly hearing from Him and my life was changing because of it. With expectancy, I would rise early every morning to be all alone with God before everyone was awake. To this day, I still cherish my time alone with God - where I speak and He listens, and where He speaks and I listen.

> *'when you pray, go into your room and shut the door*
> *and pray to your Father who is in secret.'*
> Jesus - Matthew 6:6

I did not fully abandon the journal all-together, in fact I journal quite regularly now - usually it's what I hear God speaking to me in those quiet times that I write down. Those words have become my life and breath and I refer to them often to remind myself of the things He has spoken to me. I would not be where I am today were it not for those precious times of prayer with God.

As I have thought through my personal prayer journey, I realize that it has been my daily need for God's counsel in my life that has constantly pushed me towards Him. I have literally come to find out 'I need' God in every moment of my life. I do not have peace on the inside when I do not have Him. When days go by where I don't seek His counsel through prayer, my life begins to dry up and my whole countenance goes dim.

In 1872, Annie Hawks poetically wrote of this moment by moment need for God in her hymn 'I Need Thee Every Hour';

> *I need Thee every hour, most gracious Lord;*
> *No tender voice like Thine can peace afford.*
> *I need Thee, O I need Thee;*
> *Every hour I need Thee;*
> *O bless me now, my Savior,*
> *I come to Thee.*

Learning to walk with God is not a system, it is a true relationship where we depend on Him, lean on Him, and cry out to Him in prayer. He becomes our very peace, stability, and strength as we continually go to Him. Our prayers were never meant to be a burden, they were always meant by God to be the way our soul communicates with its Creator.

Let it be so among us.

PRAYER

Oh God, I am so incredibly thankful you have given me a way to communicate with you. My soul is most happy and at peace when I am close to you. Remind me, in all circumstances, of my great need for you. My heart is only awakened by your love and daily counsel. I want to go deeper in my relationship with you, take me further God.

You are truly my life and breath.

Thank you.

Amen.

CHAPTER 11

OUR FIGHT

Ezra must rise up in this last chapter and call the people to repentance who have broken trust with God and followed their selfish ways. This is Ezra's fight.

'When pleasing men means displeasing God it is an unqualified evil and should have no place in the Christian's heart. To be right with God has often meant to be in trouble with men.'
A.W. Tozer

Against all odds, against all fears, and even against danger to ourselves - the human spirit will find a way to fight for the things it loves. I am reminded of my role as a father in protecting the hearts and minds of my children; and protecting *my own* heart from the evil in this world too. I am reminded of the importance of protecting my marriage to Sara in a culture that has decided marriage isn't valuable. I am reminded how everything I cherish would not be here today had I not fought in some way to get it here.

The fight inside each of us must be a part of our stories as well if we wish to see our lives come out of chaos. The good things in life almost always come with a fight. Now I know this is hard for those of us peacemakers, I'm one myself; we have a natural diversion to offending anyone so we default to passiveness in most situations. But if we live long enough, we will find that some situations do require our fight - in those moments we must stand in the power of our Lord Jesus and face our enemy.

What if Martin Luther King Jr. had not fought against those who wanted to keep blacks in subjection to whites? What if William Tyndale had given in to his critics and never translated the Latin Bible into English? He most surely wouldn't have been burned at the stake, but the people of his day wouldn't have had a copy of God's Word either. What if Jesus had given up when they told him to be quiet, or Peter and Paul as they began to share the gospel? What if Jeremiah had listened to his critics, kept silent and never prophesied the hope of return for the exiles we've been describing in Ezra? Sometimes life just calls for a fight, and we must rise to fulfill our God given task in those moments.

Our chief character, Ezra, had to stir up the fight in himself as well. After he took command of the returned exiles, he began to re-establish God's precious laws as described in explicit detail in the book of Deuteronomy. As he assessed the situation of his people he found that many of them were guilty of marrying into people groups who did not also believe in God; something God had warned them against. Now, I am sure Ezra just wanted to finally rest after all the work that had been done and enjoy the favor of all the people - but life often calls for so much more of us!

'And Ezra the priest <u>stood up</u> and said to them (the gathered people), "You have broken faith and married foreign women, and so increased the guilt of Israel. Now then, make confession to the Lord, the God of your fathers and do his will. Separate yourselves from the peoples of the land and from the foreign wives."'

Ezra 10:10-11

Wow - asking people to separate themselves from other people, their wives none-the-less. Calling them to confession and repentance, now that's a fight! Keep in mind, these people knew this wasn't right, they just chose to do it anyway. Deuteronomy chapter 7 talks about how God didn't want the Israelites to intermarry with people from other nations as it would turn their hearts away from Him. *(Note: Foreigners who turned their hearts to God were the exception. See Ezra 6:21 & Exodus 12:48)* But this was not an easy or popular speech for sure! It would have been much easier to just sit back and let the people be happy with their wives. But Ezra believed in something. He believed in the truth of God's Word as delivered through Moses.

I can tell you right now, Ezra was certainly not liked that day by a great many people. But Ezra had fight in him. He saw past their present situation and remembered the whole reason they were exiled in the first place was because they had abandoned God's law - he was not about to let that happen again! And you know what, the people listened to him and began to respect him for it. What I have found is that people usually respect those with fight in them - those fighting for things good and true that is.

Fights come in all shapes and sizes. Sometimes the fight must take place on the gates of your heart, where darkness lurks. The other night I was discussing this very thing with my kids before bed and we looked at Proverbs 4:23 (New International Version), 'Above all else, guard your heart, for it is the wellspring of life.' You don't guard a heart by taking life easy, you guard a heart with fierceness and determination. Sometimes it's another kind of fight - one against a sickness or injury. At other times the fight is speaking the truth in love; standing up for those things that are important like your marriage, your children, your faith, your freedom, and the freedom of those around you. Or being a voice for the poor, the elderly, and the fatherless - even when it might offend someone. You know deep inside you are fighting for something right! As John Eldredge says, *'Take anything good, true, or beautiful upon this earth and ask yourself, "can this be protected without a fight?"'*

'Our Fight' rightfully takes its place at the end of this book and in the last chapter of Ezra. You can sum up all the previous things we've been discussing, but if we won't rise up and step into the situations God has placed us in then our lives will slump back into chaos. There is something intrinsic that happens in us when we rise to the occasion; our blood gets pumping again, we remember that we are alive and called to something greater than ourselves. To choose not to fight is to choose not to live. It's a choice to sit the bench when you're being beckoned into the game.

> *'The credit belongs to the man who is actually in the arena,*
> *whose face is marred by dust and sweat and blood;*
> *who strives valiantly; who errs,*
> *who comes short again and again,*
> *because there is no effort without error and shortcoming;*
> *but who does actually strive to do the deeds;*
> *who knows great enthusiasms, the great devotions;*
> *who spends himself in a worthy cause;*
> *who at the best knows in the end*
> *the triumph of high achievement, and who at the worst,*

if he fails, at least fails while daring greatly,

so that his place shall never be with those cold and timid souls

who neither know victory nor defeat.'

Theodore Roosevelt

Ask yourself;

What has God entrusted to my care on this earth?

What is more important to me than my own life?

Determine these answers and you will have found your purpose and your fight. These are the things which are good, beautiful and true; and they are worth your fight, they are worth it every time!

<u>Prayer</u>

Not by might, not by power, but only by your Spirit can I do the things you're calling me to do. You know it's not always easy for me; but help me speak when it's time to speak and help me stand up when it's time to stand up. Fill me daily with the fullness of your Spirit and help me protect all that you have entrusted to my care.

Amen.

Epilogue

In closing I thought it fitting to end with two stories originally posted on our blog site that describe me working through some of my own places of chaos over the last few years. The first story is about the loss of my father and was written 4 months after my Dad passed away and just 6 days before our family moved to Haiti. It is about the passing on of fatherhood from one generation to the next. The second story is from a week after Christla was found unconscious and not breathing in her bed in Haiti and is about the beauty and fragility of life.

Father & Son - July 29, 2013

Four months have passed since my Dad died, yet I still find myself wanting to call him when I'm in one of my mechanical messes – he always answered those questions for me and just seemed to know what was wrong by some intuitive gift. I mean how many other people can know what is wrong with a car by listening to an engine noise over a phone call, Dad could do it (down to one or two possibilities) while I held the phone out over a running engine and wondered how this gift didn't get passed to me.

Here I am four months later going through all my Dad's old tools in his garage; my brother Josh and I reminiscing over all the amazing 'Dad fixed-it-with-this' stories – hard to believe those stories are all past now and I can't make those phone calls anymore. But it's not just the tools and the amazing mechanically minded person he was, it's as if my life at 35 years old has now entered a new and strangely different season altogether without him – like some invisible protection that was there all my life is now gone.

I feel a bit left alone in many ways, for a father gives his children that inherent covering in life no matter their age. When my Dad's father died I was a young teenager and felt loss, but there was still my Dad to look to as that buffer in front of me. All that has changed now – that protection is gone, something was taken from me that I wasn't ready to give up, things are definitely different.

And all of life becomes filled with pain and grief at times and nothing really stays the same even though we have this imaginative thought it always will – how do you move on when things change and they aren't the way they are supposed to be?

92

I think back to Eden, when all created order was perfect and there was no death or pain or struggle of life, all was perfect and as it should be. And I realize my heart was made for Eden and my heart is made for heaven; that is why my deepest self longs for things to be right again, to be REDEEMED.

> *'Meanwhile we groan, longing to be clothed instead with our heavenly dwelling.'*
> 2 Corinthians 5:2 (New International Version)

So where do I turn? Where do you turn when things aren't how they are supposed to be? Actually, I am finding my deepest joy these days in looking at my own children; how my role as father in their life has the same role my Dad's had on me, how I am that protective covering for them that my Dad was to me. And all of life goes in circles.

I find myself spending more time sitting on the floor looking at toys together – Asher is really into my old GI Joe's and we make good guy and bad guy teams and then have wars on the couch. Yesterday, Halley and Asher helped me sort through all my stashings of nuts, bolts, hooks, screws and nails. Of course, there were hooks attached to screws laying on the floor and nails in the screw compartment when we were done but I am learning to let go of such perfectness in my life to embrace THEM. Both my girls, Anna and Halley sit beside me as I type this having both just woken up – Anna is reading the Mandie Collection of books on her kindle e-reader she got for her birthday and loves to tell me how far she is in each book and how she can't put the story down because it is soooo good! Halley snuggles up by me and shows her love in that way all cuddled up in her blankie.

Yes, the loss of my Dad remains in me, but without even knowing it he showed me how to provide a fatherly covering for my own children. So, I fully step into that role the best way I know how, and in that I find God doing his redemptive work in this grief process.

God our Father making things right, God our Father redeeming the time of pain and loss, God our Father in every stage and situation of life. And I wonder why God is bringing us to the orphans of Haiti... I need wonder no longer.

'A father to the fatherless, a defender of widows is God in his holy
dwelling. God sets the lonely in families.'
Psalm 68:5-6 (New International Version)

Yon Mirak - November 7, 2015

"Yon mirak!" ("A miracle!")
I have heard this from multiple Haitian staff over the last week since Christla was found unconscious last week in her bed and ten minute later had breath in her and was alive again! Nothing short of a miracl

of God – I feel like I've dealt with things so scientifically and medically over the last week that I need to remind myself that it is God and God alone who gives us life and breath – and that night He chose to bring Christla back. I can still hear Sara's voice in my head during those frightening 10 minutes, as she called out to God to come and bring Christla back, and to heal her in Jesus name – this was no quiet prayer, this was a mother's prayer called out in desperation. And come He did!

As I think back upon the events of last week I can only come to God with a grateful heart that our little Christla – our Christla who came to us two years ago this month with no father and a mother who had just died, 5 months old, extremely under-weight, high probability she was HIV positive – this little Christla who has fought against every odd there is to fight in a country with the highest child mortality rate in the western hemisphere – this little Christla who reminds us by her very name that Christ is here with us (Christ 'la' = 'is here'), this little Christla is a walking testimony of the absolute power of God!

This morning I have been reading biblical accounts of children and others brought back to life (Elijah raising the widow's son, Jesus bringing the ruler's daughter back to life, Jesus raising the widow's son from out of a coffin, Jesus raising Lazarus from the dead, Peter healing a disciple named Tabitha who had died, Paul healing Eutychus from the dead after he fell 3 stories) and I am completely amazed and humbled at God's power and mercy to heal.

95

This little Christla has been chosen by God to display the power of God on earth!

> *'Yet He saved them for His name's sake,*
> *to make His mighty power known!'*
> Psalm 106:8 (New International Version)

I stand privileged to be called Daddy by this little girl. And while all around people are speaking of the great miracle which happened in her life, and the great glory of God's power that has been shown – I get to hold her with her little blankie as she snuggles up next to me and just be a grateful Dad!

Lord, remind us of your great work in each of our lives, remind us how much we have to be thankful for with every person around us, remind us that life is so very precious and that it is given by you for the taking and enjoying! Let this day be sacred simply because we have life and breath!

A Grateful Dad –

I hope in some small way that *all* the writings enclosed in this book will help you rise out of some place of chaos - and to God be the glory!

NOTES

Introduction

1. Henri Nouwen, *Reaching Out* (Great Britain: William Collins Sons & Co. Ltd, 1976), Foreword

Chapter 1 - Our Heart

1. Saint Augustine of Hippo, *The Confessions of Saint Augustine* (Massachusetts: Paraclete Press, 2010), p. 3

Chapter 3 - Our Relationships

1. Mother Teresa, *No Greater Love* (New York: MJF Books, 1997), p.29-30

2. Heidi Baker, *Compelled by Love* (Florida: Charisma House, 2008), p.35

Chapter 6 - Our Prophets

1. Albert Schweitzer, *Thoughts for Our Times* (Mount Vernon, NY: Peter Pauper Press, 1975), P. 16

Chapter 7 - Our Finish

1. Thomas à Kempis, *Imitation of Christ* (Massachusetts: Hendrickson Publishers, 2004), p. 62 - Note: Originally written by Thomas à Kempis in 1427 in Holland

Chapter 8 - Our Selves

1. Thomas à Kempis, *Imitation of Christ* (Massachusetts: Hendrickson Publishers 2004), p. 16

2. John Eldredge, *Fathered by God* (Nashville, Tennessee: Thomas Nelson, 2009 p. 174

Chapter 9 - Our Humility

1. J.M. Barrie, *The Little Minister* (New York: Charles Scribner's Sons, 1921), p. 27

2. Mother Teresa, *No Greater Love* (New York: MJF Books, 1997), p.6-7

Chapter 10 - Our Prayer

1. Oswald Chambers, *My Utmost for His Highest* (Grand Rapids, MI: Discover House Publishers, 1992), September 16

2. Annie Hawks, "I Need Thee Every Hour," in *Then Sings My Soul*, Robert Morgan (Nashville, TN: Thomas Nelson, 2003), p. 178

Chapter 11 - Our Fight

1. A.W. Tozer, *Man - The Dwelling Place of God,* compiled by Anita M. Baile (Camp Hill, PA: Christian Publications Inc, 1966), p. 63

2. John Eldredge, *Fathered by God* (Nashville, Tennessee: Thomas Nelson, 2009 p. 93

3. Theodore Roosevelt, *Citizenship in a Republic Speech* (Colonel Roosevelt b Edmund Morris, New York: The Random House Publishing Group, 2010), p. 4